AF674320

"Richa writes without a candle; her words, while seemingly melodic, carry underneath them a dark brooding, a certain pain and anguish that drips from every letter, every curated word. You're left with the decision of whether you want to scoop them up. If you do, you'll find yourself reading something that is delightfully pessimistic, nihilistic, at times even insolent; an unapologetic celebration of sorrow from someone who's just started what is hopefully a long voyage."

-Krishnarjun Bhattacharya, *Author of the* ***Tantric Trilogy***

"These poems are a powerful exploration of human conscience, subtly gliding between 'what is' and 'what could be'. If you are at the cusp of existential dilemma, this book will feel like home."

-Chandrama Deshmukh*, author of* ***Moonlit Monochrome.***

This is a work of fiction. Names, characters, places, and incidents are either the product of the poet's imagination or are used fictitiously. Any resemblance to actual persons, living or dead, events, locales or products, is entirely coincidental.

Paperback edition, January 2020

ISBN - 978-93-5396-807-6

Self-published by Richa Tripathi

Rose Tinted Glasses

Poems by Richa Tripathi

Self-published by Richa Tripathi
Printed by Pothi.com

To myself, for one must do things for themselves.

A note from the writer

Dear reader,

None of these poems were written while happy, and I'd like you to know that it might or might not ever be okay – but it never mattered and it never will.

Thank you for reading.

Sincerely,

Richa Tripathi

Introduction

Nothing is objectively known, or can be known, of the true nature of human conscience. Is happy and content the right way of being? Why is sadness associated with chaos?

The natural state of our very universe is darkness. The little illumination we have comes from a fiery ball hanging overhead.

Perhaps everything is not okay, and this in itself is okay?

Or perhaps, thinking this way is akin to looking through rose-tinted glasses.

Contents

Revive

Sunshine, sunshine, how will you go
to that dark, cold house
that forgot your glow?

Its roof has caved in,
the garden is bare.
The ground is swollen
and no life thrives there.

The paint is faded,
the tiles are broken,
webs adorn the ceiling,
yet not a soul's awoken.

Its pillars may crumble,

the frame could rust.

And soon become nothing,

but a mound of dust.

Sunshine, sunshine, your path is blocked.

Its doors hold strong,

they are chained

and they are locked.

Sunshine, sunshine, how will you revive,

a home so wrecked,

with air so *dry?*

Little one

Dear Stranger,

do not let your little one

wander into my arms,

lest she tumble into the abysmal depths

of this wretched soul

and lose her sunny naivety.

Or worse,

Lest her glee

lighten this heavy chest

and make it susceptible

to *purity*.

Gatoraide

The corporate world

is an energy drink.

It will charge you with temporary purpose

and move you with vigour

to some shared goal that was

never truly yours,

but never truly theirs, either.

Your love for this world

is like that too—

Two pumps of a

Gatoraide induced

Fuck.

Obstructions

Heavenly constructions,

sans sense and sound.

Formed of destruction

and entropy-bound.

Constellation formers

midnight charmers.

Silent watchers of what lives under,

made of light, silent awes, and wonder.

Heavenly constructions,

lost and found.

Stars—

but mere obstructions

to what lies *beyond.*

Victoria's secret

Let me tell you Victoria's secret—

It came from her very lips,

from the obsidian crescent of her hips.

I found her with her cigarette

standing by a lamp-lit lane,

blowing grey fumes in pure vain.

Victoria was dressed in stars and boots of animal skin.

Her charcoaled, metallic laughter mixed

with her charcoaled, metallic rings.

And she plundered into my Senses,

carved in the eternal truth.

Sweetest Victoria, in flavourful youth

Then spoke like thundering rain:

"Surely, darling. I've got a secret—

Existence is purely *pain."*

Heal

I feel a tsunami of waves in my chest,

but I must be gentle.

In spite of the maddening ringing and the tilling pain,

I must be soft, and tranquil, and gentle;

Walk as though I skip on air,

Laugh as though I'm made of bells.

I must be this,

for isn't gently how the world *heals?*

The passage of Time

"You are mine," said a Child to her heart.

"You live inside me, beat and breathe inside me.

A day will come when you will cease

and sit still, inside me.

Thus, you are mine," she concurred.

But Time had other plans,

"You are mine," said Time to the Child.

"You sleep and wake as I discern.

You will grow with me

and mature at my discretion.

It is when I blanket you,

that you will shrivel and die.

Thus, you are mine," Time concurred.

And as Time played with its toy,

the Child played with hers.

As dusk moved to dawn,

and months morphed to years,

Neither owned what once they held—

held between their *fingers*.

Give

Your fingers curl around my little heart,

and I can barely stay afloat.

The water runs over my head

and dives into my throat.

It bites and gropes, like a lover would

and I'm within its icy throes.

It wills not to make gentle love,

only wills control.

I kick and struggle to remember

if I wanted to take a swim.

Or was the water commanding

that I fulfil a decadent whim?

So oft does victory mean so less

as the will to truly live.

Does it matter that you've won me?

Or, does it matter that I *give?*

The town of the Dead

Nomad!

Wherefrom do you tread,

wandering into the town of the dead?

Here, no man is an island,

but every man is a head

bent in submission.

There are ghosts of stories untold,

haunting theses houses in remission.

In sighs, making their compensation

to opportunities lost.

Vacant and vapid, these eyes

gaze into days, passed.

Shaken by the ailing cost

of broken hearts.

Nomad!

What is it you aim to assess

amongst this hoard of corpses?

These knees are bent to mourn,

scented by that which is gone,

and in the air, disease is borne.

Oh, Nomad, bide thy time!

Leave!

Leave and never return.

Find elsewhere to sojourn.

Such times can sieve

the Light from the very skies

and any fool who thought otherwise

is now a *citizen.*

4 a.m.

The flickering
seven segment display hanging overhead
is not much of a reminder, to be honest.

I only ever wonder
"What time is it?"
when I sigh.

The City has a strange way
of making me forget
that nothing matters.

Nothing lasts against the breath of time,

and yet things can carry meanings

that we give them.

"What time is it?"

I don't know.

Could be a wintry, twelve-noon

if you kissed me right.

Could be midnight.

If I've been dreaming

of conquering the world,

Hell, maybe it's

4 am.

That which speaks to us

Luminosity is a strange phenomenon

in this world of Anti-matter

and Anti-photons

and Auntie Menons,

and Anti-bosons

(which are Bosons, in themselves)

Now somehow,

this poem has lost substance.

Like streetlamps in empty parks

and stars over empty orchids,

Without children gazing up in awe

for it is no longer

The Light

which speaks to *us*.

Strength

From where does our Strength come?

Does it come from our bones—

our bones which creak

against the boulders in our path?

Does it come from our mind?

From the indomitable spirit,

believing that hurdles are meant to be overcome

that hurdles can be overcome,

and that no hurdle is more adamant

than our resolve?

Does our Strength come from the sub-conscience,

as a by-product of being chained

by the sheer force of our oppressors?

Does it come from having strong role models
as a child?
Or from a lack, thereof?

Is it born of our most intrinsic motivations?
Or our most outrageous dreams?
Does it come from our will to live,
to feel life pulsing within us?
Or from the nihilistic knowledge
of its lack of purpose?

Maybe it is a construct of
Mind and Body.

Maybe it is the fright

of loss.

But there is one thing I know of it,

in certainty—

It is *in spite of.*

From the poet to the reader

There is no catastrophe in your life,

you should be happy—

but you don't quite comprehend

why you are not.

In fact, you are miserable

like the starved five year old

of a broken country.

Like the lover whose lover

went off to fight another's war

and never returned.

Like the tarnished good luck charm,

rubbed too often

in the name of faith.

Like the starlight which traveled light-years

only to dissolve with city-light

and become unworthy of casting shadows.

Miserable, like the writer who died

while taking a shit—

like his lost stories

and lost poetry,

never to see the light of day.

So miserable,

the Ocean proffers her colours

for perhaps, she feels her ardent blue
will do you more good
than your muted greys.

And you keep soft about it,
you don't say much.

You're that 9pm corporate
or that love-struck clerk
or the lonely librarian
or the despondent dentist
or the chemist, coffined in his coat
or any multitudes of profession.

However, the last thing

you remember being,

is *Human.*

Backstory

1. *Revive:* Revive journeys through a despondent, lonely home that once knew happiness – a reflection on the awareness of despair and the utter defeat of the spirit in its presence.

2. *Little one:* In a moment of utmost self-loathing an innocent child smiled, then looked away.

3. *Gatoraide:* Written during the months preceding my first resignation.

4. *Obstructions:* A note on being caught in the merriment of the moment, and completely losing sight of one's own goals.

5. *Victoria's secret:* Perhaps the reckless disregard towards the meaning of life is a little sexy.

6. *Heal:* Musings on an approach to make the world a better place, and the price one would have to pay for it.

7. *The passage of Time:* A story of coming of age and the losing of joie de vivre.

8. *Give:* We all have little hearts, and are selfish. Rightly so, too. In any exchange, what matters is not what can be taken from me, but what I can give.

9. *The town of the Dead:* Are any of us really alive anymore? And when we try to be, are we not defeated by the rest of us?

10. *4 a.m.:* Time is an imaginary concept. It is man-made and unnatural. Most of our memories of existence, exist outside time.

11. *That which speaks to us:* We've learned to talk in such a way that the negatives outweigh the positives.

12. *Strength:* I was thoroughly depressed and the only way I felt I could move forward was to try and figure out where my strength originates, so that I could find it again.

13. *From the poet to the reader:* It's okay to be miserable because we're human.

About the Author

Born in suburban Mumbai and brought up in parts of southern India (with a short stint in Boston, MA), Richa Tripathi has been finding her way with words since the age of eleven. Having written hundreds of poems, several short stories and many books, she decided it was time to introduce herself with *Rose Tinted Glasses*. As you read and scrutinize this paperback, Richa is wondering if you're brave enough to give despair a chance.

www.ingramcontent.com/pod-product-compliance
Lightning Source LLC
Chambersburg PA
CBHW050027170726
48282CB00025B/575
9789353968076